MARINE AIR GROUND TASK
THE PINNACLE OF COMBINED ARMS WARFARE

SCOTT CUONG TRAN AND NICK TRAN

KEY Books

Dedication
For the few, the proud, the Marines.

FRONT COVER IMAGE: A Marine squad fast-ropes down from a Bell UH-1Y Venom, ready to quickly take on any threat.

BACK COVER IMAGE: A KC-130J demonstrates its ability to refuel fast jets in mid-air, as it passes fuel to an F/A-18C Hornet and an F-35B Lightning II.

TITLE PAGE IMAGE: Using its unique vertical take-off and landing abilities, this MV-22 Osprey unloads its complement of Marines as they begin to secure the landing zone.

CONTENTS PAGE IMAGE: Marine tankers wave to the crowd at the Marine Air Ground Task Force (MAGTF) demonstration in San Diego. The demonstrations give the public an up-close and personal look at the awesome capabilities of the MAGTF.

Published by Key Books
An imprint of Key Publishing Ltd
PO Box 100
Stamford
Lincs PE9 1XQ

www.keypublishing.com

The right of Scott Cuong Tran and Nick Tran to be identified as the author of this book has been asserted in accordance with the Copyright, Designs and Patents Act 1988 Sections 77 and 78.

ISBN 978 1 80282 487 2

Typeset by SJmagic DESIGN SERVICES, India.

CONTENTS

Marine infantrymen prepare to board a Venom on their way to their next mission.

INTRODUCTION

No other military fighting force in the world has the same mystique and aura as the United States Marine Corps (USMC). Often seen as the toughest branch of the Department of Defense, since its inception in 1775, the Marines have a long and storied history of winning some of the most brutal fights. When the Continental Congress passed the Resolution Establishing the Continental Marines and "resolved that two battalions of Marines be raised," it created a service that would take its place among the most elite military units, fighting legendary battles including the Battles of New Orleans, Belleau Wood, Iwo Jima, Inchon, Khe Sanh, and Fallujah, earning and reaffirming the "Devil Dog" nickname. According to Commandant of the Marine Corps General Charles Krulakh, the mission of the USMC is simple: "For over 221 years our Corps has done two things for this great Nation. We make Marines, and we win battles."

Since its inception, the USMC has embraced its reputation for being a hard fighting, aggressive, and rugged military branch. Marines take great pride in their heritage, and it extends to all parts of their organization, from their warrior ethos to their uniforms. However, their bravado is not empty, as the Marines have centuries of victories to back up their elite status. After the vicious Battle for Iwo Jima in World War Two, Admiral Chester W. Nimitz famously said of the Marines that "Uncommon valor was a common virtue," a phrase that has been emblazoned on the US Marine Corps War Memorial in Arlington, Virginia, and exemplifies how the Marines approach their duties. No other American military branch places such a high emphasis on combat prowess as the USMC, as according to General Alfred Gray, "Every Marine is, first and foremost, a rifleman. All other conditions are secondary."

The USMC is often described as America's 9-1-1 force, ready to respond to a crisis at a moment's notice, and can field fighter jets, attack helicopters, and armored vehicles, bringing a unique ability to simultaneously dominate the air and ground battle spaces. This type of integration is critical to providing firepower from multiple domains and creating the world's premier combined arms unit, relying heavily on teamwork, training, sound doctrine, and most importantly, skilled Marines. Although mostly known for its amphibious landings, this is only a subset of the USMC core competency of being able to quickly project power anytime and anywhere. This expeditionary force projection is achieved with the Marine Air-Ground Task Force (MAGTF).

Marines use the MAGTF to rapidly deploy a self-sustaining fighting force that can accomplish a specialized mission, including amphibious landings or disaster relief. The MAGTF brings air and ground assets to the fight while also supplying important logistics, all working in unison to attack and defeat its enemy. Some MAGTF units have the capability to deploy within six hours of receiving orders, while providing all the necessary tools and firepower to open a path for traditional units to follow. It is not simply a smaller army, but rather a mobile and highly focused detachment that will allow conventional units to arrive and can maintain operations independent of local resources. This book explores the history, doctrine, and future of the MAGTF, while also showcasing the MAGTF demonstration, an annual public display of its capabilities. As the threats to liberty continue to evolve, the MAGTF concept has been changing to meet those challenges and will continue to operate as the tip of the spear for conventional American forces.

ABOVE: This LAV-25 zooms across the Miramar tarmac at a maximum speed of 60mph. Its main armament is the M242 Bushmaster 25mm chain gun, which can swivel 360 degrees on its turret.

LEFT: A Bell-Boeing MV-22 Osprey thunders overhead at Marine Corps Air Station (MCAS) Miramar. The Osprey was procured by the Marines to replace the CH-46 Sea Knight and has since participated in deployments to Afghanistan, Iraq, Kuwait, and Libya.

Although no longer part of the US Marine Corps (USMC) inventory, the M1 Abrams has played an important part in Marine battles, providing much needed firepower during the Second Battle of Fallujah. This version features a 120mm main cannon that can fire a variety of munitions for a wide variety of missions.

Marines fast-rope from a Bell UH-1Y Venom, also known as the Super Huey. In 2008, it replaced the venerable UH-1N with upgrades to nearly all desirable flight characteristics including speed, range, payload, and avionics.

CHAPTER 1

HISTORY

Operation *Starlight*

The MAGTF concept was officially introduced to USMC doctrine in 1963 when Marine Corps Order 3120.3 declared "A Marine air-ground task force with separate air ground headquarters is normally formed for combat operations and training exercises in which substantial combat forces of both Marine aviation and Marine ground units are included in the task organization of participating Marine forces," formalizing the new combined force initiative. Since then, the MAGTF has been called on to defend America and its allies, starting with the Vietnam War. One notable unit in that war was the 9th Marine Expeditionary Brigade (MEB), which landed at Da Nang in March 1965 to defend the airbase there, transitioning US involvement from an advisory to a combat role in Vietnam. It would not take long for the Marines to unleash their fighting prowess, and by August 1965, the 9th MEB successfully defended the Chu Lai Air Base against the Viet Cong 1st Regiment, inflicting heavy casualties and driving Communist forces away from the area during Operation *Starlite*. Combined arms played a major role in the Marines' victory, as A-4 Skyhawk and F-4 Phantom jets softened enemy positions with bombs and napalm as UH-1 Huey helicopters brought in troops and provided additional fire support, while M48 Patton tanks and ground troops were able to secure territory around Chu Lai Air Base. Operation *Starlite* was not only a success at fending off the Viet Cong, but it also proved the viability of the MAGTF, as

nearly every weapon system available to the Marines was utilized, including flamethrowers, helicopter gunships, and even naval gunfire. This showed that under a single commander, air, ground, and naval assets would be employed to great effect, and that "the Marines, soldiers, and sailors had performed well in what they had been trained to do: effectively utilize firepower, coordinate the use of combined arms, and kill enemy soldiers and liberate territory from enemy control." (Andrew 54) The 9th MEB set the tone for the Vietnam War, as the Viet Cong was given a tough lesson on the tenacity of the Marines and began employing guerilla-style tactics, avoiding big-unit confrontations unless absolutely necessary or favorable.

Marines advance through the broken terrain of the Van Tuong Peninsula during Operation *Starlite* on 18 August 1965. This picture is looking toward the village of Van Tuong and shows smoke from American supporting arms attacks in the background. (Photo courtesy of the USMC, photo A184945)

During the mop-up phase of Operation *Starlite*, two Marines from Company D, 1st Battalion, 7th Marines, search the area to their front for Viet Cong snipers on 22 August 1965. (Photo courtesy of the USMC, photo A185829)

Nicaragua

Although the MAGTF concept was canonized into doctrine in 1963, the use of Marine air and ground assets as a quick reaction force began almost as soon as airplanes became a viable weapon. One of the earliest uses of combined air and ground operations by the USMC occurred in Nicaragua from 1927 to 1933 in which the Marines were called upon to stabilize the country after an American had been killed by supporters of Nicaraguan revolutionary General Augusto Sandino, known as Sandinastas. After initially securing US assets and citizens, the Marines began their offensive against the Sandinistas, pushing them back on the defensive. Major Ross Rowell commanded the air squadron of de Havilland DH-4s and Atlantic-Fokker C-2s, where he

The Marines were able to train the Guardia Nacional troops, shown here together, to provide local security for Nicaragua. (Photo courtesy of the USMC)

Marines load supplies onto an Atlantic-Fokker C-2 in support of the Nicaraguan Campaign. Note on the side of the C-2 is the early eagle, globe, and anchor, which make up the USMC emblem. (Photo courtesy of the United States Army)

emphasized support for the ground troops, gaining an instant rapport with the riflemen and "this esprit de corps carried forward not only shattered the cohesiveness and morale of Sandino's insurgency, but also laid the foundation for further combined-arms integration." (Russ, p.58) Rowell's aviators supported the troops by transporting supplies, providing reconnaissance, and attacking Sandinista targets. The Marines were eventually able to provide security to ensure fair elections by 1928 and advised the indigenous Guardia Nacional, turning them into a legitimate fighting force by 1933 and allowing the Nicaraguan government to provide for its own defense. Marine actions in Nicaragua "proved that Marine aviators and infantrymen [could function] smoothly as a unified team. Thus, the MAGTF was conceived, and the resulting synergistic mechanisms of the new air-ground team provided the basis for how the MAGTF would fight in future wars." (Russ, p.64)

Fallujah

In 2004, I Marine Expeditionary Force (I MEF) took part in one of the most tenacious and toughest fights in Marine Corps history during the Second Battle of Fallujah, Iraq, which pitted combined forces from the US, UK and Iraq against thousands of insurgents holed up inside the city of Fallujah. On March 31, 2004, insurgents killed and mutilated the bodies of four American contractors and the Marines began preparations to secure the city and avenge their deaths. Preliminary operations against the insurgents began in August, which involved collecting intelligence, performing psychological and counter-intelligence operations, staging supplies, and softening up targets through bombing and artillery strikes. This mission was perfect for the MAGTF concept because all the resources needed for victory were self-contained within I MEF, including aircraft, tanks, engineers, reconnaissance, and logistics units, all of whom already trained extensively to work together as a team and had combat experience with a deployment to Iraq in the previous year. The 1st Marine Division (MARDIV) handled the ground combat element, as the 3rd Marine Aircraft Wing (MAW) covered the skies as part of the aviation combat element, while the 1st Force Support Service Group (FSSG) handled the combat support element.

In early November 2004, I MEF began offensive operations and immediately seized key roadways and bridges with a fast attack designed to minimize collateral damage and beat insurgent propaganda. The Marines pushed through the city from north to south, taking command and control hubs, communication nodes, and transportation centers. On November 13, 2004, the Marines encountered the "House of Hell," where Marines and insurgents fought to the death in extremely close quarters inside a building, resulting in one dead and 11 wounded

Americans. Two Navy Crosses were awarded for the actions at the House of Hell, the second-highest honor in the US military, one of which was earned by First Sergeant Bradley Kasal who suffered multiple gunshot wounds while protecting other injured Marines and killing at least one insurgent with his M9 pistol at close range. By the end of November, the initial assault had been completed and clearing operations began, and civilians started to return to Fallujah on December 24.

During the battle, "the Marines took control of air operations over Fallujah from the US Air Force for the battle. This…gave Marines the unity of command and control they hoped would foster efficiency and speed while minimizing fratricide," (McWilliams, p.11) showing the

An M1A1 Abrams from 2d Tank Battalion attached to 1st Battalion, 8th Marines, prepares to fire on a suspected insurgent position in Fallujah. (Photo courtesy of SSgt Jonathon C. Knauth and the USMC)

value of having a MAGTF spearheading the attack. In fact, the Marine air units out-performed the US Air Force (USAF) when it came to providing close air support during Operation *Iraqi Freedom*, "because that mission, as opposed to interdiction and strategic attack missions, is fundamental to their conception of the Marine Air-Ground Task Force." (Olsen, p.286) The results of I MEF's actions speak for themselves, as the unit killed and captured thousands of insurgents, forcing the rebels to reconstitute their forces elsewhere. By January 2005, the security situation in Fallujah had improved enough to allow for elections of a new

A CH-46E Sea Knight helicopter from Marine Medium Helicopter Squadron 268 performs a casualty evacuation for 3d Battalion, 5th Marines, on November 10, 2004. Marine rotary-wing assets provided critical support throughout the Second Battle of Fallujah. (Photo courtesy of LCpl Ryan B. Bussle and the USMC)

government, and although there would be intense combat operations in the future, I MEF proved that the MAGTF concept was still effective in an urban environment.

Operation *Steel Dawn II*

After its outstanding performance during the Second Battle of Fallujah, I MEF continued to add to its campaign streamers by participating during Operation *Steel Dawn II* to eliminate a Taliban command and logistics hub in Bahram Chah, Helmand Province, Afghanistan. From October 28 to 31, 2010, I MEF stormed into the Taliban stronghold, seizing over 20 tons of explosives along with a myriad of weapons, ammunition, drugs, and improvised explosive devices. In addition to the immediate military impact, Operation *Steel Dawn II* had a significant psychological impact on the Taliban, as the Marines conveyed the message that "We will go into the Bazaar of Barham Chah and... we'll come here anytime we want — you can't stop us. You don't get to operate with impunity," according to Lt. Col. Scott Leonard, commander of the 1st Light Armored Reconnaissance Battalion. As is tradition, the Marines acquitted themselves well in combat and sustained no casualties while cutting off a vital supply route for the Taliban. Sticking to the MAGTF concept, the ground element was led by the 1st Light Armored Reconnaissance Battalion, the aviation element was flown by the 3rd MAW, and logistics were provided by Combat Logistics Battalion 3. USAF and Marine assets provided close air support, but due to the risk of dust storms obscuring visibility, the artillery elements of the MAGTF were called on to provide firepower when aircraft were grounded. Operation *Steel Dawn II* was yet another vindication of "I MEF's aggressiveness as well as the operational utility of the Marine air-ground task force." (Lowrey, p.6)

Marines from the 1st Light Armored Reconnaissance Battalion look on as they clear enemy positions in Helmand Province during Operation *Steel Dawn II.* (Photo courtesy of GySgt Ismael Pena and the USMC).

Lance Cpl. Ryan Loving, a heavy equipment operator, Motor Transport Company B, Combat Logistics Battalion 3, 1st Marine Logistics Group (Forward), offloads supplies from an Osprey to Marines of 1st Light Armored Reconnaissance Battalion at a forward landing support area. (Photo courtesy of Cpl Paul Zellner and the USMC)

A Lockheed Martin F-35B Lightning II from VMFA-211 "Wake Island Avengers" Squadron takes off, ready to destroy targets in the air and on the ground in support of Marine infantrymen. The Wake Island Avengers transitioned from the AV-8B Harrier to the Lightning II in 2016.

CHAPTER 2
STRUCTURE

The strategic value of the MAGTF is that it brings all the vital components of combat under one umbrella, so that when called upon, it can deploy rapidly and bring the full might of the Marine arsenal to bear. For instance, if the US Army needs to move a battalion halfway across the globe, it would require an immense amount of coordination between the Army, Navy, and Air Force just to transport the troops and equipment. The USAF would also need to deploy its aircraft to provide air superiority in support of the ground units, adding another layer of complication that could cause further delays. With the MAGTF, the transportation, air support, and logistics have already been established and compounded by training and, as a result, can deploy within a matter of hours. Facilitating this efficient fighting force is the structure that consists of a command element (CE), a ground combat element (GCE), an aviation combat element (ACE), and a logistics combat element (LCE).

As the name would imply, the CE relays orders to the other elements and contains the MAGTF headquarters. No matter the size of the MAGTF, the CE provides "the command and control capabilities necessary for effective planning, execution, and assessment of operations" (MCDP 1-0) and can also serve as the headquarters for a joint task force of multi-service and multi-national units. Intelligence, reconnaissance, engineering, and radio elements from naval components can also be attached to the CE as the mission requires.

Army General John Pershing famously noted that the "deadliest weapon in the world is a Marine and his rifle!" Hyperbole aside, only a soldier with boots on the ground can take and hold territory, making the infantryman the key to a successful military operation. These ground troops are grouped into the GCE, in which they range in size from two dozen Marines to an entire division, giving the GCE the flexibility to accomplish any mission. The GCE can charge into battle using light armored vehicles, amphibious assault craft, or the omnipresent High Mobility Multipurpose Wheeled Vehicle, known affectionately as the Humvee.

The crew of this Abrams is all smiles as they wave to an adoring crowd during a Marine Air-Ground Task Force (MAGTF) demonstration. Parading these vehicles gives the public a better appreciation for the power of the Abrams, as the ground rumbles when the tank rolls by.

An LAV-25 and a Humvee roll down the tarmac in front of a cheering crowd. The LAV-25 has a crew of three, commander, gunner, and driver, and can carry up to six Marines as passengers in the rear compartment. Occupants are protected by armor rated to stop 7.62x39mm rounds from the AKM assault rifle series.

Providing air cover is the ACE, which controls the skies above the battlespace and includes fixed-wing, rotary-wing, and unmanned aircraft. To provide timely and effective support for the GCE, the ACE is flexible enough to "operate from ships or from austere expeditionary locations ashore and can readily transition between them without loss of capability." (MCDP 1-0) Marine aviation has earned much of its fame through its air-to-air exploits, but it is equally capable in the realms of electronic warfare and reconnaissance.

A column of Marine vehicles makes its way across MCAS Miramar. Convoys like these fought hard in Afghanistan and Iraq, enduring ambushes and roadside bombs, but were able to achieve victory through training and an indomitable warrior spirit.

A three-ship formation of Marine helicopters includes a Sikorsky CH-53E Super Stallion, Bell AH-1Z Viper, and a Bell-Boeing MV-22 Osprey. Although an airshow demonstration, Marine aviators often train with dissimilar airframes so they can perform integrated air operations without missing a beat.

This KC-130J of VMGR-352 "Raiders" Squadron takes off from MCAS Miramar. The Raiders provide aerial refueling capabilities to air operations. The pods below the KC-130J contain fuel needed to keep Marine aircraft aloft.

An F/A-18C Hornet from VMFA-232 "Red Devils" soars overhead. The Red Devils are one of the oldest and most storied USMC squadrons, fighting since World War Two.

The MV-22 Osprey is a unique design with tilt-rotors that allow it to land like a helicopter but it can travel as quickly and with the range of a fixed-wing aircraft, allowing the Osprey to move more equipment and troops into a combat zone faster than legacy helicopters.

After overcoming serious initial development issues, including some fatal accidents, the Osprey has amassed over 500,000 flight hours since its introduction in 2007. It serves in the US military as well as the Japanese Self Defense Force.

Although the fighting units tend to grab the headlines, the GCE and ACE would not be able to sustain the fight without the LCE, which supplies the required food, ammunition, and fuel to keep the Marines moving forward. The LCE also keeps the vehicles running by maintaining and providing general engineering support. During humanitarian missions or disaster relief, the LCE takes center stage in a MAGTF operation, showcasing its ability to handle any situation in war and peace.

CHAPTER 3

UNITS

There are three main types of MAGTFs: Marine Expeditionary Force (MEF), Marine Expeditionary Brigade (MEB), and Marine Expeditionary Unit (MEU), with two additional MAGTFs that are used for special missions: MEF Forward (MEF Fwd) and Special Purpose MAGTF (SP-MAGTF). Each has a unique role in the combat theater, with the MEF able to sustain major campaigns while the SP-MAGTF takes on more contingency operations.

The largest MAGTF is the MEF, which can have as many as 40,000 Marines and sailors and is responsible for fighting and winning large campaigns across multiple theaters. It is comprised of a Marine Division (MARDIV), a Marine Air Wing (MAW), and a Marine Logistics Group (MLG) as well as a command headquarters. There are currently three MEFs, I, II, and III, which are stationed in California and Arizona, the Carolinas, and Japan, respectively. Other units have also

I MEF logo

II MEF logo

III MEF logo

attached themselves to MEFs during major operations, including the 3 Commando Brigade from the United Kingdom. The MEF is designed to sustain itself for 60 days, and external supplies can add additional mission time. The tip of the spear of the MEF is the MEF Fwd, which can be used as a standalone MAGTF.

The MEB is the next level of MAGTF, with 16,000 troops; its role is to force entry into hostile territory, allowing follow-on forces to arrive. The subordinate groups include an infantry regiment, an aviation group, and a logistics regiment that collectively can operate for 30 days on their own. There are five MEBs currently stationed around the world and stand ready to assimilate with additional units to provide more firepower. MEBs provide amphibious assault capabilities as well as the full gamut of aviation missions.

Sailing aboard Navy Amphibious Ready Groups (ARGs) are the MEUs, the most forward-deployed MAGTF, capable of supplying security presence around the world at a moment's notice. The MEU provides stability and deterrence to hotbed regions, training local allies to provide their own defense. There are seven MEUs, and they consist of an infantry battalion, aviation squadron, and logistics battalion. They carry enough supplies for 15 days and can deploy for up to seven months with additional Naval logistics.

The SP-MAGTF serves when an MEU is unable or unavailable to perform specialized missions, such as the rapid defense of the American Embassy compound in Baghdad in January 2020. One of the hallmarks of the SP-MAGTF is its readiness level, and it can begin deployment within hours, necessitating well-planned preparations and minimalistic supply requirements and travels by air, land, or sea. SP-MAGTFs also serve as ambassadors for the Marines by linking up with regional partners to support allies.

The Kearsarge Amphibious Ready Group (ARG) trains off the East Coast for a simulated strait transit in 2010 (Photo courtesy of the United States Navy).

Special Purpose MAGTF (SP-MAGTF) Marines from 2nd Battalion, 7th Marines, reinforce the US Embassy in Baghdad, Iraq, in 2020. (Photo courtesy of Sgt. Kyle C. Talbot and the USMC)

An F/A-18C and F-35B are about to be being refueled by a KC-130J, which can offload over 40,000lbs of fuel using the probe-and-drogue system. Aerial refueling is key to providing air superiority over ground troops so that support aircraft can loiter in the area.

CHAPTER 4
STRATEGY

One of the basic tenets of USMC strategy is the concept of maneuver warfare, which exploits an enemy's weaknesses and centers of gravity, rather than attrition warfare in which victory is achieved by wearing down an enemy. Instead of committing all its forces at an enemy's strength, the Marines would rather take away its enemy's ability to continue the fight by outthinking and out maneuvering it. Striking enemy command and communication centers or supply lines could prove more decisive on the battlefield than simply killing as many enemy combatants as possible. However, that is not to say that the Marines are afraid of a fight, "On the contrary, firepower is central to maneuver warfare. Nor do we mean to imply that we will pass up the opportunity to physically destroy the enemy. We will concentrate fires and forces at decisive points to destroy enemy elements when the opportunity presents itself and when it fits our larger purposes (Warfighting)." Most associate modern maneuver warfare with USAF Colonel John Boyd, whose trademark OODA (observe, orient, decide, act) loop formed the foundation for *Warfighting*, the Marines signature doctrine document.

Most decisions, civilian and military, are made using the OODA loop, in which a person will gather the necessary data they think is relevant, position themselves to be able to take that action, make the decision, and finally act on their choice. For instance, when a hockey player is advancing the puck, they observe what the defense is doing and how their teammates are situated. The player orients themselves to a position where they can see if they should pass, shoot, or handle the puck themselves. Once the player has taken in this information, they might decide to pass to a teammate if they are uncovered. The player then acts on this decision and passes the puck. This completes the OODA loop for this decision, and the faster the player can go through the OODA loop, the more effective they will be during the game. The opposing team, however, seeks to disrupt and get inside this OODA loop by showing the player a unique defensive formation to increase the observation time or by pushing the player to disorient them. This example can be easily translated to a military decision in which a commander observes the enemy through intelligence gathering, orienting the troops to face their threat, deciding on the right tactic, and giving the order to execute.

The OODA loop can be sped up through rigorous and consistent training, allowing that hockey player or military commander to use their experiences to reduce the time needed in each step of the loop. No matter the situation, "in order to win, we should operate at a faster tempo or rhythm than our adversaries — or, better yet, get inside [the] adversary's Observation–Orientation–Decision–Action time cycle or loop. Such activity will make us appear ambiguous (unpredictable) thereby generate confusion and disorder among our adversaries — since our adversaries will be unable to generate mental images or pictures that agree with the menacing as well as faster transient rhythm or patterns they are competing against." (Boyd, p.22) Tempo, however, is not simply about acting as quickly as possible, but rather making the right decisions before the enemy can react. It is impossible to always maintain full operational speed, so the commander needs to understand when to rest and recover their forces.

An MV-22 prepares to take off from MCAS Miramar. The Osprey can transition from vertical to horizontal flight in as little as 12 seconds and can reach speeds of up to 305kn, besting the next fastest helicopter by 50kn.

The AH-1Z Viper, often referred to as the "Zulu," was developed from the AH-1W Super Cobra and sports upgraded avionics, targeting systems, safety, and a new rotor system. The Viper retains the Cobra's lethality, with a 20mm three-barreled cannon in the nose and six hardpoints for missiles and rockets.

The key to maneuver warfare is that the commander's intent is clearly communicated to his subordinates. Maneuver warfare relies on decisions to be made at the lowest level so that individual Marines can seize the initiative without asking for orders. To win battles, Marines "must understand the overall mission, and the ultimate goal of that mission—the Commander's Intent. Junior leaders must be empowered to make decisions on key tasks necessary to accomplish that mission in the most effective and efficient manner possible." (Willink, p.183) This helps get inside the enemy's OODA loop, because the Marines will act faster, forcing their opponent to react and become defensive. No battle plan can accurately predict every enemy action, so it is incumbent on the Marine on the ground to make smart decisions within the framework of the commander's intent and to adapt to the unknown. In many militaries, the commander's orders are to be followed exactly, and in the absence of orders, soldiers will simply stay put because the overall goal has not been communicated. However, through rigorous training and a robust doctrine that emphasizes the need for individual action, the Marines have been able to win wars by relying on their enlisted corps and junior officers to make the right decisions while under fire.

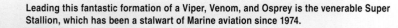

Leading this fantastic formation of a Viper, Venom, and Osprey is the venerable Super Stallion, which has been a stalwart of Marine aviation since 1974.

CHAPTER 5
MAGTF DEMONSTRATION

To display their capabilities, the MAGTFs around the country will put on airshows, complete with tanks, helicopters, fast jets, and of course, pyrotechnics. The MAGTF demonstrations have occurred at Marine Corps Air Station (MCAS) Miramar, Cherry Point, Beaufort, Yuma, and Kaneohe Bay. The MAGTF demonstration is an exciting show that simulates a MAGTF assaulting an airfield and exhibits their many capabilities all working together. These demonstrations are particularly popular because the public can get hands-on experience with some of the equipment, including handling firearms and sitting inside armored vehicles. It also provides a unique opportunity to find prospective Marines, as the show is much livelier than a recruiter's office. Perhaps the most important part of the show are the many war veterans who come to the demonstration to tell their stories at the exhibition halls, a group that are unfortunately becoming increasingly rare.

The MAGTF demonstrations are also a great way for the neighbors to see what a Marine base is all about. Because the Marines work with, and depend on, their community, investing in good relations is essential for smooth operations. At the end of the day, the Marines serve the American people, so it is important for the base to have the support of nearby residents. Additionally, the demonstrations may provide extra work and money for the locals, as tourists from around the world visit their towns to see the MAGTF in action. All in all, the Marines try to use these demonstrations as an open house and goodwill gesture towards the citizens they rely on.

Other military branches are also invited to participate in the airshow, with the US Navy Blue Angels, US Army Black Knights, and US Air Force Heritage Flight in attendance along with many civilian performers. With such an action-packed show, it is often difficult to see everything at the MAGTF demonstration, so attending multiple shows is necessary to see all that the Marines have to offer.

To take the best photographs, buying tickets at the show center is a must, and even though the cost might be high, the money will go to a good cause to support the airshow and Marines. Another way to snap unique pictures is to obtain a media pass by contacting airshow officials, but be sure to ask several months in advance because spots fill up quickly.

OPPOSITE: Aerial refueling tankers, such as this KC-130J, often take off before other aircraft in order to provide the maximum range for Marine aviators. An aircraft might take off with a minimum amount of fuel so it can get off the runway and refuel immediately to be able to make it to the target with a large payload.

"First to Fight" is seen on the port fence of this Red Devil F/A-18C, which is a vertical flat plate mounted near the leading edge of the wing. The leading edge of the F/A-18 famously allows the Hornet to fly with a high angle of attack, a significant advantage in a dogfight. However, the leading edge also caused vortices to form and impact the vertical stabilizers behind it, so much so that early Hornets received structural damage to their tails.

To prevent this damage to the tail, fences were mounted on both sides of the aircraft, seen here with the motto "Last to Leave." These fences broke up the leading edge vortices and reduced stress on the tail. Later Super Hornets solved this problem with vents that opened during high angles of attack, also breaking up these vortices.

Hornets are notoriously difficult to fight against because they can fly with extremely high angles of attack, allowing them to turn tighter and get inside an opponent's turn circle.

While the Hornet is an outstanding dogfighter, it can also deliver a heavy payload, as seen here with its weapons pylons on the wings. Although empty here the Hornet can hold up to nine hardpoints, including two wingtip missile launchers carrying a myriad of weapons, including nuclear weapons such as the B83.

The F/A-18C also flew with the Blue Angels, the Navy's flight demonstration team, from 1986 to 2020, making it the longest tenured aircraft with the team. It has since been replaced by the Super Hornet.

Although retired, the Hornet has left a lasting legacy, making it the embodiment of the multi-role fighter, performing missions ranging from fleet defense to close air support, and suppression of enemy air defenses.

On January 17, 1991, two Navy F/A-18Cs shot down two Iraqi MiG-21s while en route to a bombing mission. The pilots simply switched from air-to-ground to air-to-air modes, destroying the enemy aircraft with missiles, without having to jettison their bombs. This engagement showed the Hornet's ability to defend itself from enemy fighters while still accomplishing an air-to-ground mission.

Day or night, the Hornet has the capability to fight and win against enemies in the air and on the ground. In 1989, the Hornet received upgrades to its night-fighting capabilities, ensuring it is lethal 24 hours a day.

Teamwork is an essential part of every Marine's training. By flying in pairs, these Hornets can watch each other's 6 O'clock while increasing radar coverage when searching for targets.

The Hornet has been used by a number of countries including Canada, Australia, Switzerland, and Finland, a testament to its versatility and lethality.

The vapor cone seen from the Hornet is caused when the aircraft approaches the speed of sound and compresses the air around it, forcing the vapor moisture out of the air and creating the cone.

Inside the Hornet's nose is the venerable AN/APG-73 radar, which can track targets in the air and scan and produce high-resolution maps for terrain and ground targets.

The Hornet is powered by two General Electric F404 engines that can produce up to 18,000lbs of thrust and has a combat range of approximately 400 miles.

As the world's first production tilt-rotor aircraft, the MV-22 Osprey can land and take off vertically like a helicopter and transition to forward flight as a turboprop airplane. Therefore, no runway is required for Osprey operations.

The Osprey's primary mission is assault support in which Marine aviators airlift supplies and personnel onto the battlefield. This provides rapid mobility to the MAGTF, an essential part of the maneuver warfare doctrine.

Initially, the Osprey was plagued by design flaws and maintenance issues, causing 33 accidents and 42 deaths since its initial flight in 1989 and the date it became operational in 2007. Since then, flight components and software have been updated to reduce these issues.

Each aircraft provides over 6,000hp and can fly with one engine in an emergency. The nacelles on each wing house the engine as well as the gearboxes and accessories required to rotate the propellers.

The Osprey has three hydraulic systems and flight control computers as well as four generators that are interconnected for maximum redundancy, allowing it to continue to fly and fight even after sustaining damage.

The Marines have completely divested from their M1 Abrams tanks, sending them to the US Army to allow for lighter and faster vehicles to take their place. There were four tank battalions until 2021.

In order to lift heavy equipment such as artillery and vehicles, the CH-53E Super Stallion is powered by three General Electric T64 engines producing 4300 horsepower each, with a maximum external payload of 36,000lbs.

This fantastic formation showcases the KC-130J refueling an F-35B with F/A-18Cs in line waiting their turn. Aerial refueling is an essential part of combat missions so that aircraft have the range necessary to accomplish their mission.

With aerial refueling, an aircraft's range becomes dependent only on the pilot's endurance. The Marines have chosen to use the probe-and-drogue system in which the receiver aircraft inserts a probe into a basket connected to the refueling hose.

After refueling, the hose is retracted into the pod, helping reduce drag. The Marines use the probe-and-drogue system instead of a flying boom because their aircraft are not as large as the US Air Force's and therefore need less fuel. The boom can offload more fuel faster than the probe-and-drogue, essential for extending the range of large bombers and cargo aircraft.

Aerial refueling is also used in ferrying aircraft across oceans. Long-distance trips can be accomplished with the support of aerial tankers, which is a faster method than landing to refuel or by shipping the aircraft. Tankers are therefore considered force multipliers and essential to any combat operation.

These two Abrams are seen racing down the tarmac at MCAS Miramar. As seen on the port side of the turret, they are carrying spare tracks and wheels for the tread.

After showcasing their combat prowess, the tanker crews soak in the praise from cheering fans during an MCAS demonstration. The tank tracks use a combination of rubber and steel for the best combination of speed, mobility, and traction.

An LAV-25 and two Humvees wave to an exuberant crowd, escorted by a Marine with an M4 rifle with an M203 grenade launcher attached. Infantry and armored vehicles must work together for mutual support, with dismounted troops clearing the way for armored vehicles that can engage heavy enemy equipment.

The **F-35B** is the Marines' premier multi-role fighter jet, first introduced operationally in 2015, with its first combat strike in September 2017 against Taliban targets in Afghanistan. In Afghanistan, F-35Bs were deployed at temporary bases near enemy engagement zones, allowing the aircraft to respond immediately to threats, but also increasing the danger to the aircrew.

The option to deploy the F-35B closer to troops engaged in contract provides key advantages, and, supported by other aircraft such as the MV-22, which bring in supplies, the Lightning II helps increase the amount of firepower available to the infantryman.

The F-35B is a fifth-generation fighter, meaning that stealth has been designed into the aircraft from its initial conception. This allows the Lightning II to get closer to its targets before it is detected, increasing its stand-off abilities and survivability.

Aside from being an extremely capable fighter, the F-35B is equipped with the latest sensors and communication technologies so that it can act as a forward air battle manager, finding and assigning targets to friendly forces. This gives the Marines a first-look, first-kill advantage that can be passed on to fourth-generation fighters.

The most unique aspect of the F-35B is that it is capable of Short Take-Off and Vertical Landing (STOVL), and this Marine pilot is putting those abilities on full display. To take advantage of this feature, the engine nozzle is rotated downwards and a fan behind the cockpit opens, pushing air downwards.

While in a hover, the F-35B can also rotate, as seen in this series of photos. Additional vents and fans on the sides of the aircraft also open up to provide stability as the F-35B is suspended in mid-air.

The F-35B is the world's only fifth-generation fighter capable of STOVL. It replaces the venerable AV-8B Harrier II as the Marine's STOVL aircraft, with huge advantages in speed, payload, avionics, and of course, stealth.

This awesome head-on shot shows all of the open vents and deflected control surfaces that allow the Lightning II to seemingly float. A computer assists the pilot in making micro adjustments required for a steady hover.

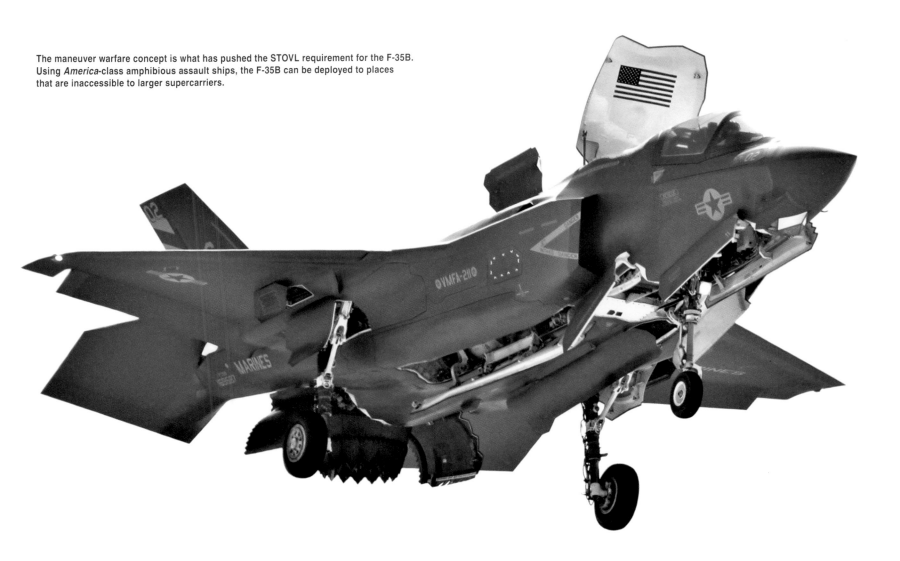

The maneuver warfare concept is what has pushed the STOVL requirement for the F-35B. Using *America*-class amphibious assault ships, the F-35B can be deployed to places that are inaccessible to larger supercarriers.

The *America*-class ships can carry up to 20 F-35Bs depending on mission requirements as well as a full complement of amphibious assault craft, including landing craft and their crew. The F-35B is part of a team that can project serious power with nearly everything needed to establish a beachhead.

Alongside the USMC, the UK and Japan both use the F-35B variant for their carrier fleets. In 2021, VMFA-211 sent ten of its F-35Bs to the HMS *Queen Elizabeth* to work with the Royal Navy and improve interoperability through a seven-month deployment to the Pacific.

The STOVL capabilities of the F-35B are perfect for the ski-jump-style carriers used by many other countries, as it allows a navy to operate a powerful fifth-generation fighter without requiring a super carrier.

The F-35 airframe is shaping up to be one of the most widely distributed aircraft, with 16 total allied countries procuring thousands of F-35s. This gives the USMC and its partners the ability to win high-intensity fights against any enemy.

This MV-22 Osprey bears down on its landing zone, ready to deliver vital troops and supplies to the combat area. The Osprey is hardy enough to enter the most highly contested areas and accomplish its mission.

An incoming Osprey is seen head-on in this photo, which showcases the fantastic and unique tilt-rotor feature. In addition to the rotor, the wings of the Osprey can rotate over the fuselage for more compact storage.

Providing the perfect background to the Blue Angels is this Osprey coming in for landing. During the MCAS demonstration, the Blue Angels stop by to show off their aerobatic skills by flying in tight formations and exact maneuvers.

Crew members are seen observing and notifying the pilots of any dangers that may impede landing. Teamwork is crucial to mission success and safety, and more lookouts increases the situational awareness for the pilots.

Exhaust "jellies" are seen emanating from the twin tilt-rotors as this Osprey touches down. As the hot air leaves the engine, it distorts the air around it and bends the light that goes through the heated air, leaving a jelly-like image.

Members of the helicopter community often joke that the rotors of their aircraft "beat the air into submission," and the Osprey's six 38-foot diameter blades certainly live up to this saying. The blades are made of a blend of polymers and composites.

This Osprey is from VMM-362, known as the "Ugly Angels," with the motto "Semper Malus" ("Always Ugly"). The Ugly Angels served in Vietnam, Afghanistan, and Iraq, flying heavy lift with the CH-53 Sea Stallion in South East Asia and with the Osprey in the Middle East.

By tilting the rotor at a 45-degree angle, the Osprey can roll on take-off and landing, allowing for increased payload. Short take-offs require less power than vertical departures, which can be used to carry additional weight.

Landing near the Red Arrows, this Osprey showcases the Marine's willingness and capability to partner with international allies in defense of freedom. The Red Arrows are the Royal Air Force's aerial demonstration team and fly the BAE Systems Hawk.

A crew member is seen observing the MAGTF demonstration from the open rear hatch. Troops and cargo are loaded and unloaded from the back ramp.

As of 2022, the Marines have received over 100 F-35s with an additional 400 more planned for delivery by 2029. As the number of F-35 orders increase, the flyaway cost of each aircraft reduces, costing less than some fourth-generation fighters such as the Eurofighter Typhoon and Dassault Rafale, making the Lightning an economical and capable defense solution.

The F-35B is the first and only aircraft with STOVL capabilities that can also break the sound barrier. Along with its array of advanced electronics and weaponry, the F-35B can accomplish any mission while still being able to land on a small footprint on a carrier.

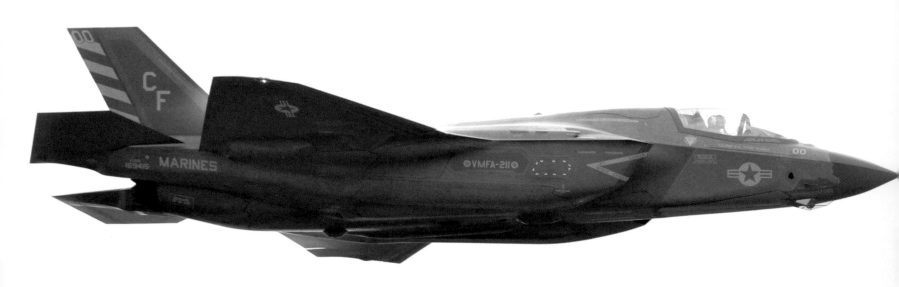

F-35s have flown more than 500,000 hours around the world in over more than 300,000 sorties and are currently stationed at over 25 bases and ten carriers.

These Marines are fast-roping from their UH-1Y Super Huey. Fast-roping is performed when troops need to quickly disembark at a location where the helicopter cannot touch down. It is faster and more dangerous than rappelling, and is used extensively to board ships and in urban environments.

A 1.5in rope is dropped from the helicopter and is weighted down in the core to prevent it from whipping around from the rotor wash. This technique was first used by the British during the Falklands War.

Fast-ropers will typically wear two layers of gloves with the first layer providing heat resistance during the descent. The first layer is then removed to improve dexterity, while the second layer provides protection during tactical work.

These Marines are also using their feet to control their descent. This is reminiscent of sliding down a firefighter's pole and gives the fast-roper additional stability and reduces some pressure on their hands.

After landing, these Marines spread out to provide perimeter security as their aircraft leaves. The ropes are released from the helicopter and later collected as the situation allows. When the Marines first touchdown, they are at their most vulnerable, so they must set up their defenses to assess the situation before moving out.

No Marine ever fights alone, and while the fast-ropers touch down, this Viper patrols overhead, looking for any danger to the infantryman. This one-two punch of helicopters keeps the enemy on their heels, having to deal with dual threats from the air and ground.

With the Viper patrolling overhead, the Marines on the ground can call for close air support to suppress or eliminate any targets. The Viper can employ a wide variety of weaponry, allowing it to defeat any adversary.

With their mission accomplished at the MAGTF demonstration, these Marines get ready to board their Super Huey, while still providing perimeter security for their teammates and aircraft.

With all Marines safely on board, the Super Huey speeds away from the target area. Flying at a maximum speed of 164kn, the Super Huey can whisk Marines to and from their destinations in a hurry.

No matter the situation, the Marines will always have each other's backs, evidenced by this Viper escorting the departing Super Huey out of the target area.

The Viper became operational with the Marines in 2010, and replaced the Super Cobra in 2020. The Czech Republic originally ordered four Vipers for its air force, and increased the order by another 12 in response to Russia's 2022 invasion of Ukraine. The Royal Bahraini Air Force has also ordered 12 Viper airframes.

The Viper can reach speeds in excess of 160 knots and has a range of more than 350 miles.
It can carry a variety of weapons including AIM-9 Sidewinder air-to-air missiles and AGM-114
Hellfire air-to-ground missiles.

The sphere on the nose of the Viper is known as the Target Sight System (TSS), which provides fire control, providing electro-optical and infrared imaging. The TSS can rotate on a gimbal and assists the pilots in detecting and locking targets.

The Viper shares 85 percent of its components with the Super Huey, making maintenance and logistics easier. Maintainers can be easily trained on both airframes, allowing for increased readiness. The Viper's parts are also resistant to saltwater corrosion, making it the perfect helicopter for offensive operations at sea.

The Viper features two General Electric T700 engines that produce over 1,800hp each, spinning four composite rotor blades that provide resistance to incoming rounds. The engine and blades are a significant improvement to the Super Cobra's power plant, as it is more reliable, easier to maintain, and provides more power.

One of the most breathtaking performers at the MAGTF demonstration are the US Navy's Blue Angels, which include Marine pilots. Marine pilots are highly skilled and among the best in the world.

Framed by two Blue Angels, an Osprey makes a landing on the tarmac at MCAS Miramar. One of the main draws of the MAGTF demonstration is the ability to see many different types of aircraft in one air show and to watch as they fly together in unique formations.

A squad of Marine riflemen disgorge from an Osprey, ready to take on any challenge. The Osprey can transport a total of 24 fully equipped Marines, bringing well-trained and motivated troops to the battlefield.

This squad begins to fan out and create a security perimeter around their aircraft, ensuring the rest of their fellow Marines can disembark safely. These exercises at the MAGTF demonstration showcase the Marines' ability to rapidly deploy with a large and capable force.

Providing additional support for the just-landed Marines is this LAV-25, racing down the tarmac of MCAS Miramar. The combined arms tactics of the Marines ensures mutual support and coverage for any weaknesses of any unit. Armored vehicles are particularly vulnerable to hand-held anti-tank weapons and rely on infantry to clear those threats, while fending off opposing enemy armor that could overwhelm infantry with heavy firepower.

One of the most exciting portions of the MAGTF demonstration is the pyrotechnics. Here, a close air support mission with a "wall of fire" is simulated behind the Blue Angels, much to the delight of the crowd.

Helo trio! Supporting the ground troops at the MAGTF demonstration is this formation including an Osprey, Super Stallion, and Viper.

These heavy lifters are key to providing logistical support to the MAGTF. Without resupplies of Marines and provisions, the fight cannot be sustained, making the Osprey and Super Stallion essential helicopters.

The Osprey can adjust its nacelles in flight for increased performance and efficiency, depending on the situation. Its ability to adjust on the fly makes it a perfect transport for the MAGTF.

This flypast of four Marine helicopters features the Stars and Stripes being flown from the UH-1Y Venom. Since 1775, the Marines have been defending America and her interests, triumphing over some of the toughest enemies and conditions in history.

The F-35B carries all of its weapons internally to reduce its radar signature. It can carry a combination of missiles, bombs, and long range stand-off weapons. When stealth is not a priority, external pylons can be mounted to carry additional payload.

The crowd at the MAGTF demonstration is awed by an F-35B hovering near the Blue Angels.
The roar of the engine and lifting fan is deafening and the ground trembles during its hover.

Special landing deck plates are required on ships that handle the F-35B because of the heat and blast force that the engine emits during a vertical landing. The temperature from the F-35B engine can reach up to 1,700°F and standard concrete or asphalt surfaces are unable to withstand the heat.

Amphibious assault ship decks are layered with a heat-resistant coating that is applied to specific landing spots for the F-35B. The special coating is a mixture of aluminum and ceramics, protecting the decks and the ship's structural integrity.

A crowd fawns over the crew of an M1A2 Abrams tank at the MAGTF demonstration at MCAS Miramar. Although the Abrams is no longer in use by the Marines, its service in the Gulf War and War on Terror has been exceptional.

This M1A2, nicknamed *Varsity*, raises its 120mm cannon in salute to the crowd. The Abrams sports an M256A1 smoothbore gun and holds up to 42 cannon rounds. Its secondary weapons include the Browning M2HB heavy machine gun and two M240 machine guns.

Beginning service with the Marines in 1983, the LAV-25 is slated to stay on with the Corps until 2035, and has seen action in Panama, Afghanistan, Haiti, and Iraq, proving its combat mettle.

The MAGTF demonstration gives civilians a chance to see the latest military technology up close. The lifting fan cover is opened to showcase this F-35Bs loyalty to the US.

Although scheduled to be replaced by the F-35B, the AV-8B Harrier II has served admirably and will continue to be with the Marines until 2029. The Harrier II validated STOVL technology and tactics while being an outstanding platform for both air-to-ground and air-to-air combat.

A very patient Marine watches as one of the authors poses with an M240B machine gun, no doubt wondering if the author will hurt himself lifting the heavy weapon. Allowing the public to handle front-line equipment gives civilians an appreciation for the strength of the Marine infantryman. The M240B weighs 27lbs unloaded and is cumbersome to carry at the MAGTF demonstration, and it would be exponentially more difficult with a full combat load in a hot and hostile environment. The Marines are indeed a hardy bunch.

The F-35 has an electro-optical targeting system under the nose, which is protected by sapphire glass. The F-35 can track targets both in the air and on the ground along all spectrums of light.

CHAPTER 6
FUTURE

As the threats to freedom continue to change, so too must the MAGTF evolve. The Marines have often been accused of being a "smaller Army" because of the simplistic perception that they take on a similar mission of engaging in land battles. While often working alongside the Army, the Marines and the MAGTF concept have the distinction of being able to take the fight to the enemy with an emphasis on the combined arms aspect of combat, meaning that the land, sea, and air components are treated in a synergistic fashion to achieve victory. Although MAGTF units have historically included heavy armor such as the M1 Abrams Main Battle Tank (MBT), the Marines have transitioned to lighter, more mobile, and lower payload vehicles, such as the Joint Light Tactical Vehicle (JLTV) with a greater emphasis on transportable unmanned aerial systems (UAS). This transition is being made in response to deadlier and higher-tech threats from China, Russia, North Korea, and other extremist organizations that have access to long-range, stand-off weapons as well as improved surveillance capabilities. With these new weapons, coupled with relatively inexpensive drones, slower and heavier formations are increasingly vulnerable to area denial systems, making traditional force-on-force and maneuver warfare more difficult. As a result, the MAGTF must counter these threats by spreading out and distributing its forces more efficiently.

Flexibility is one of the core competencies of the MAGTF, and the Marines have had to improvise, adapt, and overcome during the Global War on Terror (GWOT). For decades, they had trained to fight the Soviets who fielded massive formations of tanks, artillery, and soldiers, but as the GWOT kicked off, the Marines transitioned to counterinsurgency (COIN) operations, which are drastically different from conventional battles. Combating an insurgency requires intelligent Marines to make the right decisions on the ground in the heat of battle, as COIN has vastly more gray areas than a traditional fight. As always, the Marines can handle this new type of war with professionalism and honor, distinguishing themselves in battle and adapting to major changes. The Marine Corps continues to stay relevant, even as the GWOT dies down and new theaters of operations emerge.

Tensions in the South China Sea are beginning to set the stage for the next major battleground, as "China's aggressive actions in the South China Sea [include] building islands in order to lay claim to 1.4 million square miles of water through which approximately three trillion dollars of trade flows each year." (McMaster 91) China continues to build these islands in the face of international protest, and while they are ostensibly being built for humanitarian purposes, the US Navy has observed military equipment and personnel deployed on these artificial islands. In a March 2022 encounter, a patrolling US Navy P-8A Poseidon was warned to leave the area around the Spratly Islands in which military airfields and ports have been built by the Chinese People's Liberation Army. According to US Navy Admiral John Aquilino, "The function of those islands is to expand the offensive capability of the PRC beyond their continental shores. They can fly fighters, bombers plus all those offensive capabilities of missile systems," making these islands a potential flashpoint to a larger conflict.

To address the growing dangers in the Pacific, the Marines, under the leadership of Commandant General David Berger, are forging ahead with Force Design 2030, which will enhance their expeditionary capabilities. A lighter and more mobile force means that an MEU can deploy faster, possibly reaching its destination before enemy forces can arrive. Instead of attempting to dislodge an entrenched enemy from an island like during World War Two, the Marines are now looking to set up defensive positions on Pacific islands before the enemy can even stage their soldiers. As a result, the USMC has begun shedding some of its heavy armor, such as the M1 Abrams, as the logistical requirements for a main battle tank is significantly more complicated than light armor and infantry. Quick-responding Marines will be able to provide both tactical and strategic gains, as "forward deployed naval expeditionary forces create positional and temporal advantage for the fleet and joint force." (Force Design 2030)

Although primarily a tanker, the KC-130J can be used for offensive missions with the Harvest HAWK package, which attaches a targeting pod and Hellfire missiles. In 2010, a Harvest HAWK-equipped KC-130J engaged insurgents in Afghanistan, killing five enemy combatants during a firefight with Marines.

This magnificent formation shows the awesome capability of Marine aviation in which multiple aircraft types can work together to provide air cover and close air support for the troops on the ground.

Two F/A-18C Hornets from the Red Devils fly overhead. Although flying for the Marines, these Hornets take off and land on Navy aircraft carriers, so training with other branches is essential to interoperability.

Although it might appear that discarding some heavy weaponry would make the Marines less lethal, different capabilities such as the use of drones, F-35B aircraft, offshore support, and better intelligence gathering will enhance their ability to apply firepower. Interestingly, Force Design 2030 places an equal emphasis on the logistical requirements as the kinetic competencies, acknowledging the importance of being able to sustain the fight.

Of course, making doctrinal changes of this magnitude is not without controversy. One of the biggest criticisms of Force Design 2030 is that by discontinuing the use of heavy tanks, the capabilities of the Marines are more limited as they would be unable to go toe-to-toe with a heavy armored force. During the Second Battle for Fallujah, Abrams tanks were able to support Marines in contact by destroying fortified buildings and providing cover. Without these vehicles, the Marines would have to rely on the Army for armor, complicating operations. Another area of concern is the overreliance on technology, as Force Design 2030 envisions drones, sensors, and loitering munitions to make up for the loss of firepower. These technologies may not be as reliable as an old-fashioned tank, and there is concern that they may be come jammed or otherwise defeated. Finally, the overall downsizing of the USMC means its troops will not be able to cover as much ground and hold as much territory as a larger force. Smaller units are less resilient to losses and therefore become more vulnerable to casualties. Unfortunately, there are no easy answers to these issues, and in the face of new threats and dwindling budgets, the Marine Corps must make difficult choices. Although the doctrine, strategy, and equipment may change, one thing will remain constant and win the day: the fighting spirit and tenacity of the United States Marine.

Marine Abrams fought in Operations *Desert Storm*, *Enduring Freedom*, and *Iraqi Freedom*, enduring no combat losses while wielding an overwhelming amount of firepower in battle.

CHAPTER 7
CONCLUSION

The USMC and the MAGTF concept provide a unique capability to the American military by being a hard-hitting force that can deploy at short notice and sustain themselves until larger forces arrive. Whether it is providing humanitarian aid after a disaster or clearing a city of insurgents, the MAGTF is flexible and powerful enough to accomplish any mission, able to project American hard and soft power across the globe. General James Mattis asserted, "there is no better friend, no worse enemy than a US Marine," and the actions of his Marines have validated his claim. Public perception of the Marines as elite warriors is justified, and their combat pedigrees speak volumes to their professionalism, skill, and dedication. Their actions have time and time again shown their commitment to their country and values, making the Marines truly Semper Fidelis, Always Faithful.

With a combat load, the Viper can reach speeds in excess of 200kn and has a range of over 300 miles, bearing down on the enemy with 650 rounds of 20mm cannon, eight Hellfire missiles, and 14 70mm Hydra rockets.

FURTHER READING

Andrew, R. *The First Fight: U.S. Marines in Operation Starlite, August 1965*, Marine Corps University, History Division, (2015)

Boyd, J., & Hammond, G. T. *A Discourse on Winning and Losing*, Air University Press, (2018)

Lowrey, N., "The Raid on Bahram Chah: Operation Steel Dawn II," *Marine Corps History*, *1*(1), pp.6–23, (2015)

McMaster, H. R., *Battlegrounds: The Fight to Defend the Free World*, William Collins, (2021)

McWilliams, T., *U.S. Marines in Battle: Fallujah, November–December 2004*, Military Bookshop, (2014)

Olsen, J. A., *A History of Air Warfare,* Potomac Books, (2010)

Russ, M. The Marine Air-Ground Task Force in Nicaragua, 1927–33, Marine Corps History, 2(1), pp.55–64, (2016)

U.S. Marine Corps, *Force Design 2030: 2021 Annual Update*, (2021)

U.S. Marine Corps, *Marine Corps Doctrinal Publication 1-0: Marine Corps Operations*, (2011)

U.S. Marine Corps, *Warfighting*, (2018)

West, B., *One Million Steps: A Marine Platoon at War*, Random House, (2015)

Willink, J. & Babin, L., *Extreme Ownership: How U.S. Navy SEALs Lead and Win*, Macmillan, (2018)